Mastering MERN Stack Development: From Beginner to Pro

Chirag Meghwal

All rights reserved. No part of this book may be reproduced, distributed, or transmitted in any form or by any means, including photocopying, recording, or other electronic or mechanical methods, without the prior written permission of the publisher, except in the case of brief quotations embodied in critical reviews and certain other noncommercial uses permitted by copyright law.

This book contains content generated with the assistance of artificial intelligence (AI). While AI technology has been used to aid in the creation of certain sections of this book, the original ideas, concepts, and interpretations remain the intellectual property of the author.

For permissions requests or inquiries about the content of this book, please contact chiragmeghwal1111@gmail.com

Copyright © 2024 Chirag Meghwal

All rights reserved.

ISBN: 9798327961807

DEDICATION

This book is dedicated to all aspiring web developers who are passionate about mastering the MERN stack. Whether you're just starting your journey or seeking to enhance your skills, this book is for you.

To the learners who embrace challenges, seek knowledge, and never cease to explore the vast possibilities of web development, this dedication is a tribute to your dedication and perseverance.

May this book serve as a guiding light on your path to becoming a proficient MERN stack developer. Let your curiosity lead you, your determination fuel you, and your passion inspire you to reach new heights in your coding endeavors.

With heartfelt appreciation to all those who support and encourage the pursuit of knowledge and growth in the ever-evolving world of technology.

Happy coding!

CONTENTS

Mastering MERN Stack Development: From Beginner to Pro 0
Copyrights 1
Dedication 3
Acknowledgments 7
Chapter 1: Introduction to MERN Stack 7
    What is the MERN Stack? 7
    Advantages of the MERN Stack 8
    Getting Started with MERN Stack Development 9
Chapter 2: Setting Up Your Development Environment 12
    Installing Node.js and npm 12
    Setting Up MongoDB and Atlas 13
    Installing React and Express.js 14
    Conclusion 16
Chapter 3: Building the Backend with Node.js and Express 17
    Introduction to Express.js 17
    Creating RESTful APIs with Express 17
    Managing Data with MongoDB and Mongoose 21
    Conclusion 21
Chapter 4: Building the Frontend with React 22
    Introduction to React 22
    Getting Started with React 22
    Creating Components and Props 23
    State Management with React Hooks 24

Routing with React Router..25

Conclusion 27

Chapter 5: Integrating Frontend and Backend 28

Making HTTP Requests from React 28

Handling Authentication in React Applications 30

Building a Complete MERN Stack Application 34

Error Handling and Validation..36

Error Handling:..37

State Management with Redux 38

Testing 39

Documentation 40

Security Enhancements...40

Optimizations 41

DevOps and CI/CD 41

Analytics and Monitoring 41

Chapter 6: Advanced Topics 42

Server-Side Rendering with Next.js 42

Real-Time Communication with WebSockets 44

GraphQL and Apollo Client Integration 46

Conclusion 51

Chapter 7: Deployment and Best Practices 52

Deploying Your MERN Application to Heroku..............52

Performance Optimization Techniques.............................55

Security Best Practices and Common Vulnerabilities.............56

Conclusion 59

Chapter 8: Practical Projects and Case Studies 60

Project 1: E-commerce Platform 60

  Project 2: Social Media Application 61
  Project 3: Task Management Tool 62
  Case Study: Scalable Blogging Platform 63
  Conclusion 65
Chapter 9: Conclusion and Next Steps 66
  Recap of Key Concepts 66
  Next Steps for Further Learning 68
  Conclusion 69
From the Author 71

ACKNOWLEDGMENTS

I would like to take this opportunity to express my gratitude to all those who have supported me in the creation of this book.

First and foremost, I extend my heartfelt appreciation to the team at Amazon. Your dedication and support have been instrumental in bringing this project to fruition.

I am deeply thankful to my family and friends for their unwavering encouragement and understanding throughout this endeavor. Your belief in me has been a source of strength and inspiration.

I would also like to extend my gratitude to the online communities, forums, and resources that have provided valuable insights and assistance along the way. Your contributions have enriched my understanding and enhanced the quality of this book.

Finally, I extend my heartfelt thanks to the readers who have chosen to embark on this learning journey with me. Your interest and support are truly appreciated.

Thank you to everyone who has played a part, no matter how big or small, in making this book a reality.

Chapter 1: Introduction to MERN Stack

Welcome to "Mastering MERN Stack Development: From Beginner to Pro"! In this chapter, we'll dive into the fundamentals of the MERN stack, a powerful set of technologies for building modern web applications.

What is the MERN Stack?

The MERN stack is a full-stack JavaScript framework that consists of four main components:

1.MongoDB:

MongoDB is a NoSQL database that stores data in flexible, JSON-like documents. Unlike traditional relational databases that store data in tables and rows, MongoDB uses collections and documents, providing greater flexibility in handling data.

MongoDB supports a rich query language and provides features like indexing, aggregation, and replication, making it suitable for a wide range of applications.

2.Express.js:

Express.js is a minimalist web framework for Node.js that simplifies the process of building web servers and APIs. It provides a robust set of features for building single and multi-page web applications.

Express.js handles routing, middleware, and HTTP requests, allowing developers to create scalable and maintainable web applications with ease.

1. **React:**

React is a JavaScript library for building user interfaces, developed by Facebook. It allows developers to create reusable UI components and manage the state of their applications efficiently.

React's virtual DOM (Document Object Model) enhances performance by updating only the parts of the UI that have changed, rather than re-rendering the entire page.

2. **Node.js:**

Node.js is a runtime environment for executing JavaScript code server-side. It uses an event-driven, non-blocking I/O model, making it lightweight and efficient for building scalable network applications.

Node.js allows developers to use JavaScript for server-side scripting, enabling the creation of dynamic web pages before they are sent to the client's browser.

Advantages of the MERN Stack

The MERN stack offers several advantages for web developers:

1. **Single Language:**

With JavaScript powering both the frontend and backend, developers can write code using a single language. This unified language environment streamlines development and improves productivity, as developers do not need to switch between different languages.

2. **Full Stack Development:**

The MERN stack enables developers to work on both the frontend and backend of web applications. This full stack capability provides greater control and flexibility over the entire development process, allowing for more cohesive and integrated solutions.

3. **Rich Ecosystem:**

Each component of the MERN stack has a rich ecosystem of libraries, frameworks, and tools. This extensive ecosystem makes it easy to extend and customize your development environment, providing solutions for a wide range of use cases and challenges.

4. **Real-Time Updates:**

Using technologies like WebSockets and React's virtual DOM, developers can create real-time web applications with instant updates and notifications. This capability is essential for applications like chat apps, live dashboards, and collaborative tools.

Getting Started with MERN Stack Development

To get started with MERN stack development, you'll need to have a basic understanding of JavaScript and web development concepts. Here's a step-by-step guide to help you begin your journey:

1. **Set Up Your Development Environment:**

Install Node.js and npm (Node Package Manager) from the official website (https://nodejs.org). npm comes bundled with Node.js and is used to manage project dependencies.

Install MongoDB from the official website (https://mongodb.com). MongoDB provides the database for your application.

2. **Learn the Basics of Each Component:**

MongoDB: Familiarize yourself with MongoDB's basics, such as creating databases, collections, and documents. Learn how to perform CRUD (Create, Read, Update, Delete) operations.

Express.js: Learn how to set up a basic Express.js server, handle routes, and use middleware for handling requests and responses.

React: Understand the fundamentals of React, including components, state, props, and lifecycle methods. Learn how to create and manage a React application.

Node.js: Learn the basics of Node.js, including its asynchronous nature, event loop, and how to interact with the file system and other modules.

3. **Build a Simple MERN Application:**

Start with a simple project, such as a to-do list or a blog application. This project will help you understand how the different components of the MERN stack work together.

Set up a MongoDB database and create a schema for your data.

Create an Express.js server to handle API requests and interact with the MongoDB database.

Build a React frontend to interact with your Express.js backend, displaying data from MongoDB and handling user interactions.

4. **Explore Advanced Topics**:

Once you're comfortable with the basics, explore advanced topics such as authentication, state management with Redux, server-side rendering with Next.js, and real-time communication with WebSockets.

In the next chapter, we'll cover setting up your development environment and installing the necessary tools to start building MERN stack applications.

Chapter 2: Setting Up Your Development Environment

In this chapter, we'll guide you through the process of setting up your development environment for MERN stack development. By the end of this chapter, you'll have all the necessary tools installed and configured to start building MERN stack applications.

Installing Node.js and npm

Node.js and npm (Node Package Manager) are essential for MERN stack development. Node.js allows you to run JavaScript code on the server side, while npm helps you manage project dependencies.

Steps to Install Node.js and npm:

1. **Download and Install:**

Visit the official Node.js website (https://nodejs.org) and download the installer for your operating system.

Follow the installation instructions. The installer will include npm automatically.

2. **Verify Installation:**

Open your terminal or command prompt.

Run the following commands to verify the installation:

```bash
node -v
npm -v
```

These commands should display the installed versions of Node.js and npm.

Setting Up MongoDB and Atlas

MongoDB is a NoSQL database that stores data in JSON-like documents. For this book, we'll use MongoDB Atlas, a cloud-based database service that simplifies the setup and management of MongoDB databases.

Steps to Set Up MongoDB Atlas:

1. **Create an Account**:
    - Go to the MongoDB Atlas website (https://www.mongodb.com/cloud/atlas) and create a free account.
2. **Create a Cluster**:
    - After signing in, create a new cluster. Choose the free tier option for testing and learning purposes.
3. **Configure Your Cluster**:
    - Add your IP address to the whitelist to allow access to the database.
    - Create a database user and set a password.
4. **Connect to Your Cluster**:

Obtain the connection string for your cluster. It will look something like this:

```php
mongodb+srv://<username>:<password>@cluster0.mongodb.net/<dbname>?retryWrites=true&w=majority
```

Replace <username>, <password>, and <dbname> with your actual username, password, and database name.

Installing React and Express.js

React and Express.js are crucial for the frontend and backend of your MERN stack application.

Installing React:

1. **Create a New React Application**:

Use Create React App, a comfortable environment for learning React and building a new single-page application:

```bash
npx create-react-app my-app
cd my-app
npm start
```

This will create a new React application and start the development server. Open http://localhost:3000 in your browser to see the default React app running.

Installing Express.js:

1. **Create a New Express Application**:

Create a new directory for your backend application and navigate into it:

```bash
mkdir my-express-app
cd my-express-app
```

Initialize a new Node.js project:

```bash
npm init -y
```

Install Express.js:

```bash
npm install express
```

Create a simple server:

```javascript
// Create a file named app.js
const express = require('express');
const app = express();
const port = 3001;

app.get('/', (req, res) => {
  res.send('Hello, world!');
});

app.listen(port, () => {
  console.log(`Server is running on http://localhost:${port}`);
});
```

- Run your Express server:

```bash
Copy code
node app.js
```

- Open http://localhost:3001 in your browser to see the message "Hello, world!".

Conclusion

In this chapter, you set up your development environment for MERN stack development by installing Node.js and npm, configuring MongoDB Atlas, and installing React and Express.js. With these tools in place, you're now ready to start building your MERN stack applications.

In the next chapter, we'll dive into building your first MERN stack application by setting up the backend with Express.js and MongoDB.

Chapter 3: Building the Backend with Node.js and Express

In this chapter, we'll focus on building the backend of your MERN stack application using Node.js and Express. We will start by introducing Express.js, then create RESTful APIs, and finally manage data with MongoDB using Mongoose.

Introduction to Express.js

Express.js is a fast, unopinionated, minimalist web framework for Node.js. It simplifies the process of building robust and scalable web applications by providing a set of powerful features for handling HTTP requests, routing, middleware, and more.

Key Features of Express.js:

- **Routing**: Defines how your application responds to client requests to different endpoints.
- **Middleware**: Functions that execute during the lifecycle of a request to the server, enabling features like logging, authentication, and error handling.
- **Template Engines**: Integrates with template engines like Pug, EJS, and Handlebars to generate HTML dynamically.
- **Static Files**: Serves static files such as images, CSS, and JavaScript easily.

Creating RESTful APIs with Express

RESTful APIs are a way to create web services that allow clients to communicate with your server using HTTP methods such as GET, POST, PUT, and DELETE. We'll create a simple API for a to-do list application.

Setting Up the Project:

1. **Initialize a New Project**:

```bash
mkdir todo-app
cd todo-app
npm init -y
npm install express mongoose
```

2. **Create the Server File**:

```javascript
// Create a file named server.js
const express = require('express');
const mongoose = require('mongoose');
const app = express();
const port = 3000;

// Middleware to parse JSON requests
app.use(express.json());

// Connect to MongoDB
mongoose.connect('your_mongodb_connection_string', { useNewUrlParser: true, useUnifiedTopology: true })
  .then(() => console.log('Connected to MongoDB'))
  .catch(err => console.error('Could not connect to MongoDB', err));

// Define a route
app.get('/', (req, res) => {
  res.send('Hello, world!');
});

// Start the server
app.listen(port, () => {
  console.log(`Server is running on http://localhost:${port}`);
});
```

3. **Run the Server:**

```bash
node server.js
```

Defining the API Endpoints:

1. **Create a To-Do Model:**

    javascript

    ```
    // Create a file named models/todo.js
    const mongoose = require('mongoose');

    const todoSchema = new mongoose.Schema({
      title: { type: String, required: true },
      completed: { type: Boolean, default: false }
    });

    const Todo = mongoose.model('Todo', todoSchema);

    module.exports = Todo;
    ```

2. **Create the API Routes:**

    Javascript

    ```
    // Add the following routes to server.js
    const Todo = require('./models/todo');

    // Get all to-dos
    app.get('/todos', async (req, res) => {
    try {
    const todos = await Todo.find();
    res.json(todos);
    } catch (err) {
    res.status(500).send(err);
    }
    });

    // Get a single to-do by ID
    ```

```javascript
app.get('/todos/:id', async (req, res) => {
try {
const todo = await Todo.findById(req.params.id);
if (!todo) return res.status(404).send('To-do not found');
res.json(todo);
} catch (err) {
res.status(500).send(err);
}
});

// Create a new to-do
app.post('/todos', async (req, res) => {
try {
const todo = new Todo({
title: req.body.title,
completed: req.body.completed
});
await todo.save();
res.status(201).json(todo);
} catch (err) {
res.status(400).send(err);
}
});

// Update a to-do by ID
app.put('/todos/:id', async (req, res) => {
try {
const todo = await Todo.findByIdAndUpdate(req.params.id,
req.body, { new: true, runValidators: true });
if (!todo) return res.status(404).send('To-do not found');
res.json(todo);
} catch (err) {
res.status(400).send(err);
}
});

// Delete a to-do by ID
app.delete('/todos/:id', async (req, res) => {
try {
const todo = await Todo.findByIdAndDelete(req.params.id);
if (!todo) return res.status(404).send('To-do not found');
res.send('To-do deleted');
} catch (err) {
res.status(500).send(err); }});
```

Managing Data with MongoDB and Mongoose

Mongoose is an Object Data Modeling (ODM) library for MongoDB and Node.js. It provides a straightforward, schema-based solution to model your application data.

Setting Up Mongoose:

1. **Defining Schemas**:

Schemas define the structure of the documents within a collection. For example, in the to-do application, the todoSchema defines that each to-do item will have a title and a completed status.

2. **Creating Models**:

Models are constructors compiled from the schema definitions. They create and read documents from the MongoDB database.

3. **Performing CRUD Operations**:

Mongoose provides methods for performing CRUD operations on the models. These include find, findById, save, findByIdAndUpdate, and findByIdAndDelete.

Conclusion

In this chapter, you learned how to build the backend of your MERN stack application using Node.js and Express. We covered the basics of Express.js, created RESTful APIs, and managed data with MongoDB using Mongoose. In the next chapter, we'll start building the frontend using React.

Chapter 4: Building the Frontend with React

Introduction to React

React is a JavaScript library developed by Facebook for building user interfaces, particularly single-page applications where you need a fast, interactive user experience. It allows developers to create reusable UI components, manage the view layer of web applications, and handle state efficiently.

Key Features of React:

1. **Component-Based Architecture**: Encapsulates components that manage their own state and logic.
2. **Virtual DOM**: Efficiently updates and renders components, improving performance.
3. **Unidirectional Data Flow**: Data flows in one direction, making it easier to debug and understand.

Getting Started with React

To start developing with React, you need to set up your development environment and create a new React application.

Setting Up the React Environment:

1. **Create a New React Application:**

```bash
npx create-react-app my-app
cd my-app
npm start
```

- ➢ npx create-react-app my-app creates a new React application named my-app.
- ➢ cd my-app changes the directory to your new application folder.
- ➢ npm start runs the development server, which you can access at http://localhost:3000.

2. **Project Structure**:
   - ➢ public/: Contains static assets like HTML and images.
   - ➢ src/: Contains React components and other JavaScript files.
   - ➢ src/index.js: Entry point for the React application.
   - ➢ src/App.js: Main application component.

Creating Components and Props

In React, the UI is broken down into components. Each component is a self-contained piece of the UI that can be reused and composed with other components.

Creating a Simple Component:

1. **Define a Component**:

   javascript

   ```
   // src/components/Hello.js
   import React from 'react';

   const Hello = (props) => {
     return <h1>Hello, {props.name}!</h1>;
   };

   export default Hello;
   ```

2. **Using the Component in App.js:**

   javascript

   ```
   // src/App.js
   import React from 'react';
   import Hello from './components/Hello';

   function App() {
     return (
       <div className="App">
         <Hello name="World" />
       </div>
     );
   }

   export default App;
   ```

Understanding Props:

- Props (short for properties) are a way to pass data from parent to child components.
- In the example above, name="World" is passed as a prop to the Hello component.

State Management with React Hooks

State represents the dynamic parts of your application. React Hooks, introduced in React 16.8, allow you to use state and other React features without writing a class.

Using the useState Hook:

1. **Initialize State:**

   javascript

   ```
   import React, { useState } from 'react';

   function Counter() {
     const [count, setCount] = useState(0);
   ```

```jsx
  return (
    <div>
      <p>You clicked {count} times</p>
      <button onClick={() => setCount(count + 1)}>
        Click me
      </button>
    </div>
  );
}

export default Counter;
```

2. **Explanation**:
    - useState is a Hook that declares a state variable and a function to update it.
    - const [count, setCount] = useState(0) initializes count to 0.

Routing with React Router

React Router is a standard library for routing in React. It enables navigation among views of various components in a React application, changing the browser URL, and keeping the UI in sync with the URL.

Setting Up React Router:

1. **Install React Router**:

    ```bash
    npm install react-router-dom
    ```

2. **Create Routes**:

    ```javascript
    // src/App.js
    import React from 'react';
    ```

```
import { BrowserRouter as Router, Route, Switch } from 'react-router-dom';
import Home from './components/Home';
import About from './components/About';

function App() {
  return (
    <Router>
      <div className="App">
        <Switch>
          <Route exact path="/" component={Home} />
          <Route path="/about" component={About} />
        </Switch>
      </div>
    </Router>
  );
}

export default App;
```

3. **Create Components**:

   javascript

   ```
   // src/components/Home.js
   import React from 'react';

   const Home = () => {
     return <h1>Home Page</h1>;
   };

   export default Home;

   // src/components/About.js
   import React from 'react';

   const About = () => {
     return <h1>About Page</h1>;
   };

   export default About;
   ```

Explanation:

- **Router**: Wraps the entire application and enables routing.
- **Switch**: Renders the first matching route.
- **Route**: Defines a path and the component to render when the path matches.

Conclusion

In this chapter, we've covered the fundamentals of building the frontend with React. We introduced React, set up a development environment, created components and props, managed state with React Hooks, and implemented routing with React Router. In the next chapter, we'll integrate the frontend with the backend.

Chapter 5: Integrating Frontend and Backend

In this chapter, we will explore how to integrate the frontend and backend of a MERN stack application. This involves making HTTP requests from React to the Express backend, handling authentication, and building a complete MERN stack application.

Making HTTP Requests from React

To interact with your backend server from a React application, you need to make HTTP requests. This can be done using various libraries, but axios is a popular choice due to its simplicity and ease of use.

Setting Up Axios:

1. **Install Axios**:

    ```bash
    npm install axios
    ```

2. **Making GET Requests**:

    ```javascript
    // src/components/TodoList.js
    import React, { useEffect, useState } from 'react';
    import axios from 'axios';

    const TodoList = () => {
      const [todos, setTodos] = useState([]);

      useEffect(() => {
        axios.get('/api/todos')
          .then(response => setTodos(response.data))
    ```

```
      .catch(error => console.error('Error fetching todos:', error));
  }, []);

  return (
    <div>
      <h1>Todo List</h1>
      <ul>
        {todos.map(todo => (
          <li key={todo._id}>{todo.title}</li>
        ))}
      </ul>
    </div>
  );
};

export default TodoList;
```

3. **Making POST Requests**:

   javascript

   ```
   // src/components/AddTodo.js
   import React, { useState } from 'react';
   import axios from 'axios';

   const AddTodo = () => {
     const [title, setTitle] = useState('');

     const addTodo = () => {
       axios.post('/api/todos', { title })
         .then(response => console.log('Todo added:', response.data))
         .catch(error => console.error('Error adding todo:', error));
     };

     return (
       <div>
         <input
           type="text"
           value={title}
           onChange={e => setTitle(e.target.value)}
         />
         <button onClick={addTodo}>Add Todo</button>
       </div>
   ```

```
  );
};

export default AddTodo;
```

Explanation:

- **Axios GET Request**: Fetches data from the /api/todos endpoint and sets the todos state with the response data.
- **Axios POST Request**: Sends a new todo to the /api/todos endpoint and logs the response.

Handling Authentication in React Applications

Authentication is crucial for securing your application. In this section, we will implement user authentication using JSON Web Tokens (JWT).

Backend Authentication Setup:

1. **Install Dependencies:**

   ```bash
   npm install bcryptjs jsonwebtoken
   ```

2. **User Model:**

   javascript

   ```
   // models/User.js
   const mongoose = require('mongoose');
   const bcrypt = require('bcryptjs');

   const UserSchema = new mongoose.Schema({
     username: { type: String, required: true, unique: true },
     password: { type: String, required: true }
   });

   UserSchema.pre('save', async function(next) {
     if (!this.isModified('password')) return next();
   ```

```javascript
  const salt = await bcrypt.genSalt(10);
  this.password = await bcrypt.hash(this.password, salt);
  next();
});

const User = mongoose.model('User', UserSchema);
module.exports = User;
```

3. **Authentication Routes**:

javascript

```javascript
// routes/auth.js
const express = require('express');
const bcrypt = require('bcryptjs');
const jwt = require('jsonwebtoken');
const User = require('../models/User');
const router = express.Router();

// Register Route
router.post('/register', async (req, res) => {
  try {
    const { username, password } = req.body;
    const user = new User({ username, password });
    await user.save();
    res.status(201).send('User registered');
  } catch (error) {
    res.status(400).send('Error registering user');
  }
});

// Login Route
router.post('/login', async (req, res) => {
  try {
    const { username, password } = req.body;
    const user = await User.findOne({ username });
    if (!user || !await bcrypt.compare(password, user.password)) {
      return res.status(400).send('Invalid credentials');
    }
    const token = jwt.sign({ userId: user._id }, 'secret_key');
    res.json({ token });
  } catch (error) {
    res.status(400).send('Error logging in');
  }
```

});

   module.exports = router;

4. **Protecting Routes**:

   javascript

   ```javascript
   // middleware/auth.js
   const jwt = require('jsonwebtoken');

   const auth = (req, res, next) => {
     const token = req.header('Authorization').replace('Bearer ', '');
     if (!token) return res.status(401).send('Access denied');

     try {
       const decoded = jwt.verify(token, 'secret_key');
       req.user = decoded;
       next();
     } catch (error) {
       res.status(400).send('Invalid token');
     }
   };

   module.exports = auth;
   ```

Frontend Authentication Setup:

1. **Login Form Component**:

   javascript

   ```javascript
   // src/components/Login.js
   import React, { useState } from 'react';
   import axios from 'axios';

   const Login = () => {
     const [username, setUsername] = useState('');
     const [password, setPassword] = useState('');
     const [token, setToken] = useState('');

     const loginUser = () => {
       axios.post('/api/auth/login', { username, password })
         .then(response => {
   ```

```
        setToken(response.data.token);
        console.log('Logged in successfully');
      })
      .catch(error => console.error('Error logging in:', error));
  };

  return (
    <div>
      <input
        type="text"
        placeholder="Username"
        value={username}
        onChange={e => setUsername(e.target.value)}
      />
      <input
        type="password"
        placeholder="Password"
        value={password}
        onChange={e => setPassword(e.target.value)}
      />
      <button onClick={loginUser}>Login</button>
    </div>
  );
};

export default Login;
```

Explanation:

- **Backend**: User model with password hashing, registration and login routes, JWT authentication middleware.
- **Frontend**: Login form that sends a request to the backend and handles the received token.

Building a Complete MERN Stack Application

Now that we have covered the basics of making HTTP requests and handling authentication, let's combine everything to build a complete MERN stack application.

Project Structure:

- **Backend**: Node.js with Express for the server, MongoDB for the database.
- **Frontend**: React for the user interface.

Setting Up the Project:

1. **Backend Setup**:
    - Create a new Express project as shown in previous chapters.
    - Set up models, routes, and middleware for handling data and authentication.
2. **Frontend Setup**:
    - Create a new React application.
    - Set up components for displaying data and handling user interactions.

Example: Todo Application with Authentication:

1. **Backend**:
    - Define user and todo models.
    - Set up routes for authentication and todo management.
    - Implement middleware to protect routes.
2. **Frontend**:
    - Create components for login, registration, todo list, and adding todos.
    - Use axios to interact with the backend.
    - Handle user authentication and store the token.

Putting It All Together:

1. **Backend Code**:

    javascript

    ```javascript
    const express = require('express');
    const mongoose = require('mongoose');
    const authRoutes = require('./routes/auth');
    const todoRoutes = require('./routes/todos');
    const auth = require('./middleware/auth');

    const app = express();
    const port = 3000;

    mongoose.connect('your_mongodb_connection_string', { useNewUrlParser: true, useUnifiedTopology: true });

    app.use(express.json());
    app.use('/api/auth', authRoutes);
    app.use('/api/todos', auth, todoRoutes);

    app.listen(port, () => console.log(`Server running on http://localhost:${port}`));
    ```

2. **Frontend Code**:

    javascript

    ```javascript
    // src/App.js
    import React from 'react';
    import { BrowserRouter as Router, Route, Switch } from 'react-router-dom';
    import Login from './components/Login';
    import TodoList from './components/TodoList';
    import AddTodo from './components/AddTodo';

    function App() {
      return (
        <Router>
          <div className="App">
            <Switch>
              <Route path="/login" component={Login} />
    ```

```
            <Route path="/todos" component={TodoList} />
            <Route path="/add-todo" component={AddTodo} />
          </Switch>
        </div>
      </Router>
    );
}

export default App;
```

3. **Authentication and Todo Components**:
    - Handle user authentication, display todos, and allow adding new todos.
    - Use the token for making authenticated requests to protected routes.

Error Handling and Validation

Backend Validation:

- Use libraries like joi for validating request data before processing.

javascript

```
const Joi = require('joi');

const registerSchema = Joi.object({
  username: Joi.string().min(3).required(),
  password: Joi.string().min(6).required()
});

router.post('/register', async (req, res) => {
  const { error } = registerSchema.validate(req.body);
  if (error) return res.status(400).send(error.details[0].message);
  // Continue with registration
});
```

Frontend Validation:

- Validate user inputs before making API calls.

javascript

```javascript
const validateForm = () => {
  if (username.length < 3) {
    alert('Username must be at least 3 characters');
    return false;
  }
  if (password.length < 6) {
    alert('Password must be at least 6 characters');
    return false;
  }
  return true;
};
```

Error Handling:

- Handle errors gracefully both on the backend and frontend to improve user experience. **Backend Error Handling:**

javascript

```javascript
router.post('/register', async (req, res) => {
  try {
    // Registration logic
  } catch (error) {
    res.status(500).send('Internal Server Error');
  }
});
```

Frontend Error Handling:

javascript

```javascript
const loginUser = () => {
  axios.post('/api/auth/login', { username, password })
    .then(response => {
      setToken(response.data.token);
      console.log('Logged in successfully');
    })
    .catch(error => {
      console.error('Error logging in:', error);
```

```
      alert('Login failed. Please check your credentials.');
    });
};
```

State Management with Redux

For larger applications, consider using Redux for state management to maintain a predictable state container.

Setting Up Redux:

1. **Install Redux and React-Redux:**

```bash
npm install redux react-redux
```

2. **Create Redux Store:**

```javascript
// src/store.js
import { createStore } from 'redux';

const initialState = {
  user: null,
  todos: []
};

function rootReducer(state = initialState, action) {
  switch (action.type) {
    case 'SET_USER':
      return { ...state, user: action.payload };
    case 'SET_TODOS':
      return { ...state, todos: action.payload };
    default:
      return state;
  }
}

const store = createStore(rootReducer);
```

```
export default store;
```

3. **Provide Store to Application:**

javascript

```
// src/index.js
import React from 'react';
import ReactDOM from 'react-dom';
import { Provider } from 'react-redux';
import store from './store';
import App from './App';

ReactDOM.render(
  <Provider store={store}>
    <App />
  </Provider>,
  document.getElementById('root')
);
```

Testing

Implement both unit and integration testing to ensure your application works as expected.

Backend Testing:

- Use Jest and Supertest for testing Express routes.

javascript

```
const request = require('supertest');
const app = require('../app');

describe('GET /api/todos', () => {
  it('should fetch all todos', async () => {
    const res = await request(app).get('/api/todos');
    expect(res.statusCode).toEqual(200);
    expect(res.body).toHaveProperty('todos');
  });
});
```

Frontend Testing:

- Use Jest and React Testing Library.

javascript

```javascript
import { render, screen } from '@testing-library/react';
import TodoList from './TodoList';

test('renders todo list', () => {
  render(<TodoList />);
  const linkElement = screen.getByText(/Todo List/i);
  expect(linkElement).toBeInTheDocument();
});
```

Documentation

Include detailed documentation for your codebase to make it easier for others (or yourself in the future) to understand the architecture and logic.

Security Enhancements

- Implement security best practices such as rate limiting, data sanitization, and secure storage of sensitive information.

Rate Limiting:

javascript

```javascript
const rateLimit = require('express-rate-limit');

const limiter = rateLimit({
  windowMs: 15 * 60 * 1000, // 15 minutes
  max: 100 // limit each IP to 100 requests per windowMs
});

app.use('/api/', limiter);
```

Optimizations

- Optimize your application for performance, such as using lazy loading for components and efficient data fetching strategies.

Lazy Loading:

javascript

```
const LazyComponent = React.lazy(() => import('./components/LazyComponent'));

function App() {
  return (
    <Suspense fallback={<div>Loading...</div>}>
      <LazyComponent />
    </Suspense>
  );
}
```

DevOps and CI/CD

Set up Continuous Integration and Continuous Deployment (CI/CD) pipelines to automate testing and deployment processes.

Analytics and Monitoring

Integrate tools to monitor the performance and usage of your application in real time.

Example Tools:

- **Frontend**: Google Analytics, Hotjar
- **Backend**: New Relic, Sentry
-

Chapter 6: Advanced Topics

In this chapter, we will delve into more advanced topics that can significantly enhance your MERN stack applications. We will explore Server-Side Rendering (SSR) with Next.js, real-time communication with WebSockets, and integrating GraphQL with Apollo Client.

Server-Side Rendering with Next.js

Next.js is a powerful framework for React that enables Server-Side Rendering (SSR) and static site generation. SSR can improve the performance and SEO of your application by rendering the initial HTML on the server.

Setting Up Next.js

1. **Create a New Next.js Project**:

    ```bash
    npx create-next-app my-next-app
    cd my-next-app
    ```

2. **Pages and Routing**:

    Next.js uses the pages directory to define routes. Each file in this directory corresponds to a route.

    ```javascript
    // pages/index.js
    import React from 'react';

    const Home = () => {
      return <h1>Welcome to Next.js!</h1>;
    };

    export default Home;
    ```

3. **Fetching Data on the Server:**

   Use getServerSideProps to fetch data on the server side.

   javascript

   ```
   // pages/todos.js
   import React from 'react';
   import axios from 'axios';

   const Todos = ({ todos }) => {
     return (
       <div>
         <h1>Todos</h1>
         <ul>
           {todos.map(todo => (
             <li key={todo._id}>{todo.title}</li>
           ))}
         </ul>
       </div>
     );
   };

   export async function getServerSideProps() {
     const response = await axios.get('http://localhost:3000/api/todos');
     return { props: { todos: response.data } };
   }

   export default Todos;
   ```

Explanation:

- **Next.js Project**: Start a new project with Next.js.
- **Pages and Routing**: Each file in the pages directory represents a route.
- **Data Fetching**: Use getServerSideProps for fetching data on the server side.

Real-Time Communication with WebSockets

Real-time communication allows your application to send and receive updates instantly. WebSockets are a protocol that provides full-duplex communication channels over a single TCP connection.

Setting Up WebSockets with Socket.io

1. **Install Socket.io:**

    ```bash
    npm install socket.io
    ```

2. **Backend Setup:**

    ```javascript
    // server.js
    const express = require('express');
    const http = require('http');
    const socketIo = require('socket.io');

    const app = express();
    const server = http.createServer(app);
    const io = socketIo(server);

    io.on('connection', (socket) => {
      console.log('New client connected');
      socket.on('disconnect', () => {
        console.log('Client disconnected');
      });
      socket.on('message', (message) => {
        io.emit('message', message);
      });
    });

    const port = 4000;
    server.listen(port, () => console.log(`Listening on port ${port}`));
    ```

3. **Frontend Setup:**

javascript

```javascript
// src/App.js
import React, { useEffect, useState } from 'react';
import socketIOClient from 'socket.io-client';

const ENDPOINT = "http://localhost:4000";

const App = () => {
  const [messages, setMessages] = useState([]);
  const [input, setInput] = useState('');
  const socket = socketIOClient(ENDPOINT);

  useEffect(() => {
    socket.on('message', (message) => {
      setMessages((prevMessages) => [...prevMessages, message]);
    });

    return () => {
      socket.disconnect();
    };
  }, [socket]);

  const sendMessage = () => {
    socket.emit('message', input);
    setInput('');
  };

  return (
    <div>
      <ul>
        {messages.map((message, index) => (
          <li key={index}>{message}</li>
        ))}
      </ul>
      <input
        type="text"
        value={input}
        onChange={(e) => setInput(e.target.value)}
      />
      <button onClick={sendMessage}>Send</button>
    </div>
```

```
    );
};

export default App;
```

Explanation:

- **Backend**: Set up a basic server with Socket.io for handling WebSocket connections and events.
- **Frontend**: Connect to the WebSocket server, handle incoming messages, and send messages.

GraphQL and Apollo Client Integration

GraphQL is a query language for your API that allows clients to request exactly the data they need. Apollo Client is a comprehensive state management library for JavaScript that enables you to manage both local and remote data with GraphQL.

Setting Up GraphQL with Apollo Server

1. **Install Dependencies**:

```bash
npm install apollo-server express graphql mongoose
```

2. **Define GraphQL Schema and Resolvers**:

```javascript
// server.js
const { ApolloServer, gql } = require('apollo-server-express');
const express = require('express');
const mongoose = require('mongoose');

const app = express();

// MongoDB model
```

```javascript
const Todo = mongoose.model('Todo', new mongoose.Schema({
  title: String,
  completed: Boolean
}));

// GraphQL schema
const typeDefs = gql`
  type Todo {
    id: ID!
    title: String!
    completed: Boolean!
  }

  type Query {
    todos: [Todo]
  }

  type Mutation {
    addTodo(title: String!): Todo
    toggleTodoCompleted(id: ID!): Todo
  }
`;

// GraphQL resolvers
const resolvers = {
  Query: {
    todos: () => Todo.find()
  },
  Mutation: {
    addTodo: async (_, { title }) => {
      const todo = new Todo({ title, completed: false });
      await todo.save();
      return todo;
    },
    toggleTodoCompleted: async (_, { id }) => {
      const todo = await Todo.findById(id);
      todo.completed = !todo.completed;
      await todo.save();
      return todo;
    }
  }
};
```

```javascript
const server = new ApolloServer({ typeDefs, resolvers });
server.applyMiddleware({ app });

mongoose.connect('your_mongodb_connection_string', {
useNewUrlParser: true, useUnifiedTopology: true });

app.listen({ port: 4000 }, () =>
  console.log(`Server ready at http://localhost:4000${server.graphqlPath}`)
);
```

Setting Up Apollo Client in React

1. **Install Apollo Client**:

    ```bash
    npm install @apollo/client graphql
    ```

2. **Configure Apollo Client**:

    ```javascript
    // src/App.js
    import React from 'react';
    import { ApolloProvider, InMemoryCache, ApolloClient } from '@apollo/client';
    import TodoList from './components/TodoList';
    import AddTodo from './components/AddTodo';

    const client = new ApolloClient({
      uri: 'http://localhost:4000/graphql',
      cache: new InMemoryCache()
    });

    function App() {
      return (
        <ApolloProvider client={client}>
          <div className="App">
            <TodoList />
            <AddTodo />
          </div>
        </ApolloProvider>
      );
    ```

```
}

export default App;
```

3. **Fetching Data with Apollo Client:**

javascript

```
// src/components/TodoList.js
import React from 'react';
import { useQuery, gql } from '@apollo/client';

const GET_TODOS = gql`
  query GetTodos {
    todos {
      id
      title
      completed
    }
  }
`;

const TodoList = () => {
  const { loading, error, data } = useQuery(GET_TODOS);

  if (loading) return <p>Loading...</p>;
  if (error) return <p>Error :(</p>;

  return (
    <ul>
      {data.todos.map(todo => (
        <li key={todo.id}>{todo.title}</li>
      ))}
    </ul>
  );
};

export default TodoList;
```

4. **Mutations with Apollo Client:**

   javascript

   ```
   // src/components/AddTodo.js
   import React, { useState } from 'react';
   import { useMutation, gql } from '@apollo/client';

   const ADD_TODO = gql`
     mutation AddTodo($title: String!) {
       addTodo(title: $title) {
         id
         title
         completed
       }
     }
   `;

   const AddTodo = () => {
     const [title, setTitle] = useState('');
     const [addTodo] = useMutation(ADD_TODO);

     const handleSubmit = (e) => {
       e.preventDefault();
       addTodo({ variables: { title } });
       setTitle('');
     };

     return (
       <form onSubmit={handleSubmit}>
         <input
           type="text"
           value={title}
           onChange={(e) => setTitle(e.target.value)}
           placeholder="Add a new todo"
         />
         <button type="submit">Add</button>
       </form>
     );
   };

   export default AddTodo;
   ```

Explanation:

- **Apollo Server**: Set up a GraphQL server with Express and define your schema and resolvers.
- **Apollo Client**: Configure Apollo Client in your React application to fetch and manipulate data using GraphQL.

Conclusion

In this chapter, we've covered several advanced topics that can significantly enhance your MERN stack applications:

1. **Server-Side Rendering with Next.js**: Improves performance and SEO by rendering pages on the server.
2. **Real-Time Communication with WebSockets**: Enables instant updates and interactions within your application.
3. **GraphQL and Apollo Client**: Provides a flexible and efficient way to fetch and manage data.

By mastering these advanced topics, you will be well-equipped to build sophisticated and high-performance web applications using the MERN stack.

Chapter 7: Deployment and Best Practices

This chapter focuses on deploying your MERN stack application to a production environment and discusses best practices to optimize performance and enhance security.

Deploying Your MERN Application to Heroku

Heroku is a popular platform as a service (PaaS) that simplifies the deployment process. Here, we will cover the steps required to deploy your MERN application to Heroku.

Setting Up Your Application for Deployment

1. **Create a Procfile:**

A Procfile is used by Heroku to determine how to run your application.

```plaintext
web: node server.js
```

2. **Update package.json:**

Ensure your package.json includes necessary scripts and dependencies.

```json
{
  "name": "mern-app",
  "version": "1.0.0",
  "main": "server.js",
  "scripts": {
    "start": "node server.js",
    "heroku-postbuild": "cd client && npm install && npm run build"
  },
```

```
"dependencies": {
  "express": "^4.17.1",
  "mongoose": "^5.11.15",
  "react": "^17.0.1",
  "react-dom": "^17.0.1",
  "react-scripts": "4.0.1"
 }
}
```

3. **Configure MongoDB Atlas:**
    - Use MongoDB Atlas for your database and update your connection string in server.js.

javascript

```
mongoose.connect(process.env.MONGODB_URI ||
'your_mongodb_connection_string', {
  useNewUrlParser: true,
  useUnifiedTopology: true
});
```

4. **Serve React App from Express:**
    - Modify your Express server to serve the React app.

javascript

```
const path = require('path');

app.use(express.static(path.join(__dirname, 'client/build')));

app.get('*', (req, res) => {
  res.sendFile(path.join(__dirname, 'client/build', 'index.html'));
});
```

Deploying to Heroku

1. **Login to Heroku:**

```bash
heroku login
```

2. **Create a New Heroku App:**

```bash
heroku create mern-app
```

3. **Add MongoDB Atlas Environment Variable:**

```bash
heroku config:set MONGODB_URI=your_mongodb_connection_string
```

4. **Initialize Git and Deploy:**

```bash
git init
git add .
git commit -m "Initial commit"
git push heroku master
```

5. **Open Your Deployed App:**

```bash
heroku open
```

Performance Optimization Techniques

Performance optimization is crucial for providing a fast and responsive user experience. Here are some key techniques:

1. **Code Splitting and Lazy Loading**:
    - Use React's React.lazy and Suspense to load components only when they are needed.

    javascript

    ```javascript
    const SomeComponent = React.lazy(() => import('./SomeComponent'));

    <Suspense fallback={<div>Loading...</div>}>
      <SomeComponent />
    </Suspense>
    ```

2. **Memoization**:
    - Use React.memo and useMemo to prevent unnecessary re-renders.

    javascript

    ```javascript
    const MemoizedComponent = React.memo(SomeComponent);

    const value = useMemo(() => computeExpensiveValue(a, b), [a, b]);
    ```

3. **Optimizing Images**:
    - Compress and use appropriate image formats. Serve images in WebP format for better compression.
    - Use lazy loading for images.

    ```html
    <img src="image.webp" loading="lazy" alt="Description">
    ```

4. **Minifying and Compressing Assets**:
    o Use tools like Webpack to minify JavaScript and CSS files.
    o Enable Gzip compression on your server.
5. **Database Indexing**:
    o Index frequently queried fields in MongoDB to speed up read operations.

    javascript

    ```
    mongoose.Schema({
      fieldName: { type: String, index: true }
    });
    ```

6. **Caching**:
    o Use caching strategies like Redis for frequently accessed data.

Security Best Practices and Common Vulnerabilities

Security is paramount to protect your application and user data. Here are best practices to secure your MERN stack application:

1. **Sanitize Inputs**:
    o Prevent injection attacks by sanitizing user inputs.

    javascript

    ```
    const sanitize = require('mongo-sanitize');
    const sanitizedInput = sanitize(req.body.input);
    ```

2. **Use HTTPS**:
    - Ensure your application uses HTTPS to encrypt data in transit.

    javascript

    ```javascript
    const fs = require('fs');
    const https = require('https');

    https.createServer({
      key: fs.readFileSync('server.key'),
      cert: fs.readFileSync('server.cert')
    }, app).listen(443);
    ```

3. **Environment Variables**:
    - Store sensitive data like API keys and database credentials in environment variables.

    ```bash
    heroku config:set SECRET_KEY=your_secret_key
    ```

4. **Authentication and Authorization**:
    - Use robust authentication mechanisms like JWT.

    javascript

    ```javascript
    const jwt = require('jsonwebtoken');
    const token = jwt.sign({ id: user._id },
    process.env.SECRET_KEY, { expiresIn: '1h' });
    ```

5. **Rate Limiting**:
    - Implement rate limiting to protect against brute-force attacks.

    javascript

    ```javascript
    const rateLimit = require('express-rate-limit');
    const limiter = rateLimit({
      windowMs: 15 * 60 * 1000, // 15 minutes
      max: 100 // limit each IP to 100 requests per windowMs
    ```

});

app.use(limiter);

6. **Content Security Policy (CSP)**:
    - Use CSP headers to prevent cross-site scripting (XSS) attacks.

javascript

```
const helmet = require('helmet');
app.use(helmet.contentSecurityPolicy({
  directives: {
    defaultSrc: ["'self'"],
    scriptSrc: ["'self'", "'trusted-scripts.com'"]
  }
}));
```

7. **Cross-Origin Resource Sharing (CORS)**:
    - Configure CORS to control which domains can access your API.

javascript

```
const cors = require('cors');
app.use(cors({
  origin: 'https://your-frontend-domain.com',
  methods: ['GET', 'POST']
}));
```

Conclusion

In this chapter, we covered essential topics for deploying and optimizing your MERN stack application:

1. **Deploying to Heroku**: Simplified steps to get your application up and running on Heroku.
2. **Performance Optimization**: Techniques to ensure your application runs efficiently and provides a smooth user experience.
3. **Security Best Practices**: Measures to protect your application from common vulnerabilities and attacks.

By following these best practices, you can ensure your MERN stack application is robust, secure, and performant.

Chapter 8: Practical Projects and Case Studies

In this chapter, we will explore several practical projects to solidify your understanding of the MERN stack. These projects will help you apply the concepts learned in previous chapters and provide real-world examples of how to build full-stack applications. Additionally, we will review a case study of a scalable blogging platform to illustrate best practices in MERN stack development.

Project 1: E-commerce Platform

Overview

An e-commerce platform is an online application that allows users to browse products, add them to a shopping cart, and complete purchases. Building this project will help you understand how to manage complex data relationships and implement secure payment processes.

Key Features

1. **User Authentication and Authorization**:
    - Implement user registration and login using JWT (JSON Web Tokens).
    - Differentiate between user roles (e.g., admin, customer).
2. **Product Management**:
    - Allow admins to add, edit, and delete products.
    - Enable users to browse and search for products.
3. **Shopping Cart**:
    - Allow users to add products to a shopping cart and manage quantities.
    - Persist shopping cart data across sessions.
4. **Order Processing**:

- Implement checkout and order processing workflows.
- Integrate payment gateways like Stripe or PayPal for secure transactions.
5. **User Reviews and Ratings**:
    - Allow users to review and rate products.
    - Display average ratings and reviews on product pages.

Technologies Used

- **Frontend**: React, React Router, Redux (for state management)
- **Backend**: Node.js, Express
- **Database**: MongoDB, Mongoose
- **Authentication**: JWT, bcrypt
- **Payment Processing**: Stripe or PayPal APIs

Project 2: Social Media Application

Overview

A social media application enables users to create profiles, post content, follow other users, and interact through likes and comments. This project will demonstrate how to build a dynamic and interactive application with real-time updates.

Key Features

1. **User Profiles**:
    - Allow users to create and update their profiles.
    - Display user information, profile pictures, and bio.
2. **Posts and Feeds**:
    - Enable users to create, edit, and delete posts.
    - Display a feed of posts from followed users.
3. **Likes and Comments**:
    - Implement functionality for liking and commenting on posts.

- o Display likes and comments in real-time using WebSockets.
4. **Follow System:**
    - o Allow users to follow and unfollow other users.
    - o Display a list of followers and following on user profiles.
5. **Notifications:**
    - o Implement real-time notifications for likes, comments, and new followers.

Technologies Used

- **Frontend:** React, Redux, WebSocket (for real-time updates)
- **Backend:** Node.js, Express, Socket.io
- **Database:** MongoDB, Mongoose
- **Authentication:** JWT, bcrypt

Project 3: Task Management Tool

Overview

A task management tool helps users organize their tasks, set deadlines, and track progress. Building this project will help you understand CRUD (Create, Read, Update, Delete) operations and state management.

Key Features

1. **User Authentication**:
   - Implement user registration and login with JWT.
   - Protect routes to ensure only authenticated users can access their tasks.
2. **Task Management**:
   - Allow users to create, edit, delete, and mark tasks as complete.
   - Categorize tasks by priority and due date.
3. **Project Management**:
   - Enable users to create and manage multiple projects.
   - Assign tasks to specific projects and track progress.
4. **Collaborative Features**:
   - Allow users to invite others to collaborate on projects.
   - Implement real-time updates for task changes using WebSockets.

Technologies Used

- **Frontend**: React, React Router, Redux
- **Backend**: Node.js, Express, Socket.io
- **Database**: MongoDB, Mongoose
- **Authentication**: JWT, bcrypt

Case Study: Scalable Blogging Platform

Overview

A scalable blogging platform allows multiple users to create and manage their own blogs. This case study demonstrates how to design and implement a scalable architecture for a multi-user application.

Key Features

1. **Multi-User Authentication**:
   - Implement user registration and login.
   - Differentiate between regular users and admin users.
2. **Blog Creation and Management**:
   - Allow users to create, edit, and delete blog posts.
   - Implement rich-text editing for blog content.
3. **Comment System**:
   - Enable users to comment on blog posts.
   - Display comments in real-time using WebSockets.
4. **Tagging and Categorization**:
   - Allow users to tag and categorize their posts.
   - Implement search functionality to filter posts by tags and categories.
5. **Scalability Considerations**:
   - Use a microservices architecture to separate concerns (e.g., authentication, blogging, commenting).
   - Implement caching with Redis to improve performance.
   - Use a load balancer to distribute traffic across multiple servers.

Technologies Used

- **Frontend**: React, Next.js (for server-side rendering)
- **Backend**: Node.js, Express, Microservices architecture
- **Database**: MongoDB, Mongoose
- **Authentication**: JWT, OAuth (for social login)
- **Real-Time Updates**: WebSocket, Redis (for caching)

Conclusion

In this chapter, we have explored several practical projects and a detailed case study to demonstrate the capabilities of the MERN stack. These projects provide a comprehensive understanding of how to build full-stack applications, handle real-time updates, and scale applications for production.

1. **E-commerce Platform**: Teaches complex data management and secure payment processing.
2. **Social Media Application**: Demonstrates dynamic and interactive features with real-time updates.
3. **Task Management Tool**: Highlights CRUD operations and collaborative features.
4. **Scalable Blogging Platform**: Provides insights into building and scaling a multi-user application.

By working on these projects, you will gain practical experience and be well-equipped to build sophisticated applications using the MERN stack.

Chapter 9: Conclusion and Next Steps

Congratulations on completing "Mastering MERN Stack Development: From Beginner to Pro"! In this final chapter, we'll recap what you've learned throughout the book and discuss next steps for further learning and exploration in MERN stack development.

Recap of Key Concepts

This section serves as a refresher of the fundamental concepts covered throughout the book:

1. **Introduction to MERN Stack:**

Recap of the four main components: MongoDB, Express.js, React, and Node.js.

Highlighting the advantages of using the MERN stack for full-stack web development, such as its single language (JavaScript) approach and rich ecosystem of tools and libraries.

2. **Setting Up Development Environment:**

Reiterating the process of setting up the development environment, including installing Node.js, MongoDB, and React, and configuring them for development.

3. **Building Backend with Node.js and Express:**

Reviewing the basics of Express.js and how it simplifies building web servers and APIs.

Summarizing the process of creating RESTful APIs and managing data using MongoDB and Mongoose.

4. **Building Frontend with React**:

Recapitulating the core concepts of React, including components, props, state management with React Hooks, and routing with React Router.

5. **Integrating Frontend and Backend**:

Summarizing the process of integrating frontend and backend components to create a complete MERN stack application, including making HTTP requests from React and handling authentication.

6. **Advanced Topics**:

Revisiting advanced topics covered, such as server-side rendering with Next.js, real-time communication with WebSockets, and integrating GraphQL and Apollo Client.

7. **Deployment and Best Practices**:

Summarizing the deployment process to platforms like Heroku and discussing performance optimization techniques and security best practices.

Next Steps for Further Learning

This section outlines recommended steps for continuing your learning journey beyond the scope of the book:

1. **Explore Advanced Topics:**

Encourages further exploration of advanced concepts like serverless architecture, microservices, and containerization to expand your knowledge and skill set.

2. **Build Real-World Projects:**

Suggests practicing by building more complex projects, such as social networks or e-commerce platforms, to apply and solidify your understanding of MERN stack development.

3. **Contribute to Open Source:**

Advocates for contributing to open-source projects on platforms like GitHub to collaborate with other developers and gain practical experience in real-world scenarios.

4. **Continuous Learning:**

Emphasizes the importance of staying updated with the latest trends and technologies in web development through continuous learning via blogs, tutorials, workshops, and conferences.

5. **Specialize:**

Recommends considering specialization in specific areas of web development, such as frontend, backend, or DevOps, to deepen expertise and focus on areas of interest.

Conclusion

The conclusion section wraps up the book and offers final words of encouragement and congratulations for completing the learning journey. It emphasizes the importance of continuous learning, experimentation, and improvement in becoming a proficient web developer.

Overall, Chapter 9 provides a comprehensive summary of key concepts, guidance for further learning, and encouragement to continue advancing your skills in MERN stack development.

From the Author

Thank you for embarking on this journey with me through "Mastering MERN Stack Development: From Beginner to Pro." I hope this book has provided you with the knowledge and tools needed to confidently build full-stack web applications using the MERN stack.

As a self-taught developer and independent publisher, my goal has always been to share practical insights and real-world experience to help others succeed in the ever-evolving field of web development. This book is a culmination of countless hours of learning, coding, and refining techniques to provide a comprehensive guide that is accessible to developers at all levels.

I encourage you to continue experimenting, building projects, and pushing the boundaries of what you can achieve with the MERN stack. The world of web development is vast and full of opportunities, and with perseverance and passion, you can achieve great things.

I would love to hear about your experiences, projects, and feedback on this book. Feel free to reach out to me via email at [chiragmeghwal1111@gmail.com]. Your insights and stories are invaluable and help shape future editions and new projects.

Thank you once again for your support. I wish you the best of luck on your coding journey and look forward to seeing the amazing applications you create.

Happy coding!

Chirag Meghwal

www.ingramcontent.com/pod-product-compliance
Lightning Source LLC
Chambersburg PA
CBHW031544210526
45464CB00003B/1135